Forever memorable, our journey begins on the road through Oak Creek Canyon.

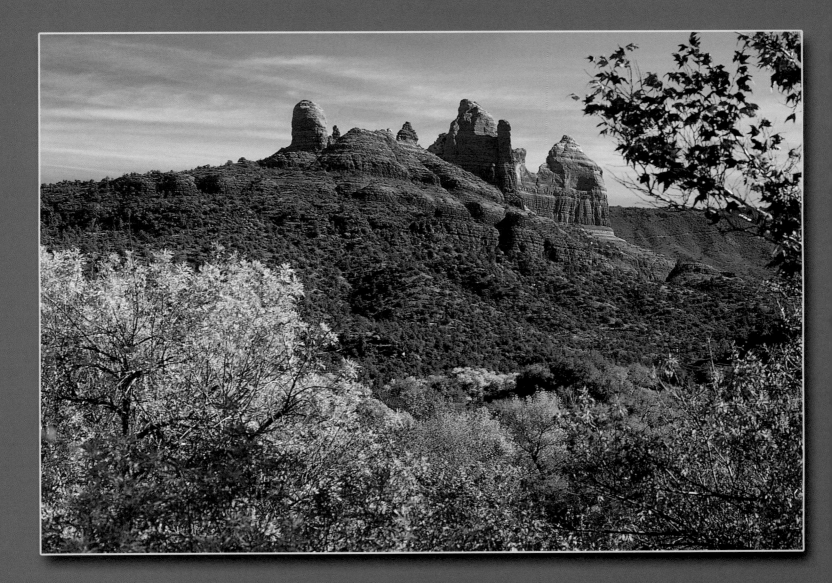

Mitten Ridge – part of the Schnebly Hill formation

Courthouse Rock stands majestically above Loop Road.
Known as Courthouse Rock for 130 years, it has also been
referred to as Cathedral Rock more recently.

Courthouse Rock has spectacular views anytime of day.

Oak Creek Falls, located just below Slide Rock in Oak Creek Canyon ...
a breathtaking sight year-round.

Fruit trees reveal their blossoms in the valley below Oak Creek Canyon.

Oak Creek at Indian Gardens is a beautiful sight with Autumn colors.

Melting snows in the Spring form tumbling waterfalls in Oak Creek Canyon.

Oak Creek Canyon
under a peaceful
winter blanket.

Oak Creek near Slide Rock, dressed in icicles and snow.

Spectacular
Schnebly Canyon
is more beautiful
than ever,
decorated
with snow
and clouds.

The west wall of
Oak Creek Canyon
is a magical site
after a light snowfall
in early December.

Picturesque farms
and ranches lay
hidden in the
lower part of
Red Rock Country.

Oak Creek
wanders through
this beautiful valley
just south of
Radisson
Poco Diablo Resort.

A mystical view
of Dry Creek
through
statuesque
pines.

Crystal clear
red rock streams
are created by
melting snow
from the
high country.

Pendley Arch is the most colorful of arches in red rock country.

Devil's Bridge is located in the Dry Creek area just north of Sedona.
It spans 45 feet across and towers 55 feet above the canyon floor.

Fay Canyon Arch spans 94 feet on the east wall of Fay Canyon.

Red Rock
Crossing
in the
peak color
of Autumn.

Snow decorates
Oak Creek in this
January scene of
Red Rock Crossing.

Atop
Schnebly Hill
Road you can
see a vast
panorama.

In 1949, Bob Bradshaw captured this never-to-be-seen again moment as Charlie Brewer drove his cattle down a dirt road towards Bell Rock.

This same road, now Highway 179, is paved today
and leads millions of tourists to Sedona.

Bell Rock in Autumn with a dance of wild sunflowers.

Bell Rock stands in her summer mood.

Sacred Datura

Cream Cups

Fendler Rose

Narrowleaf Sunflower

Butterfly Weed

Yellow Ragweed

Paper Flower

Sedona
wild flowers
in the Spring
against a
prickly pear cactus
background.

37

Tlaquepaque was
built by Abe Miller
and completed in 1982.
It is one of the most
unique attractions
in Sedona.

Tlaquepaque's Chapel and courtyard
portrays the flavor of Old Mexico.

Snoopy Rock,
at the end of Camel Rock
was captured by
Bob Bradshaw's son,
John Bradshaw.
This rare shot was taken
when storm clouds broke
for that critical few seconds,
allowing John the opportunity
to continue the Bradshaw heritage
of exceptional photography.

Courthouse Rock
is silhouetted in
this spectacular
sunset photo.

Colorful
Coffee Pot Rock
is the background
of this
West Sedona
scene.

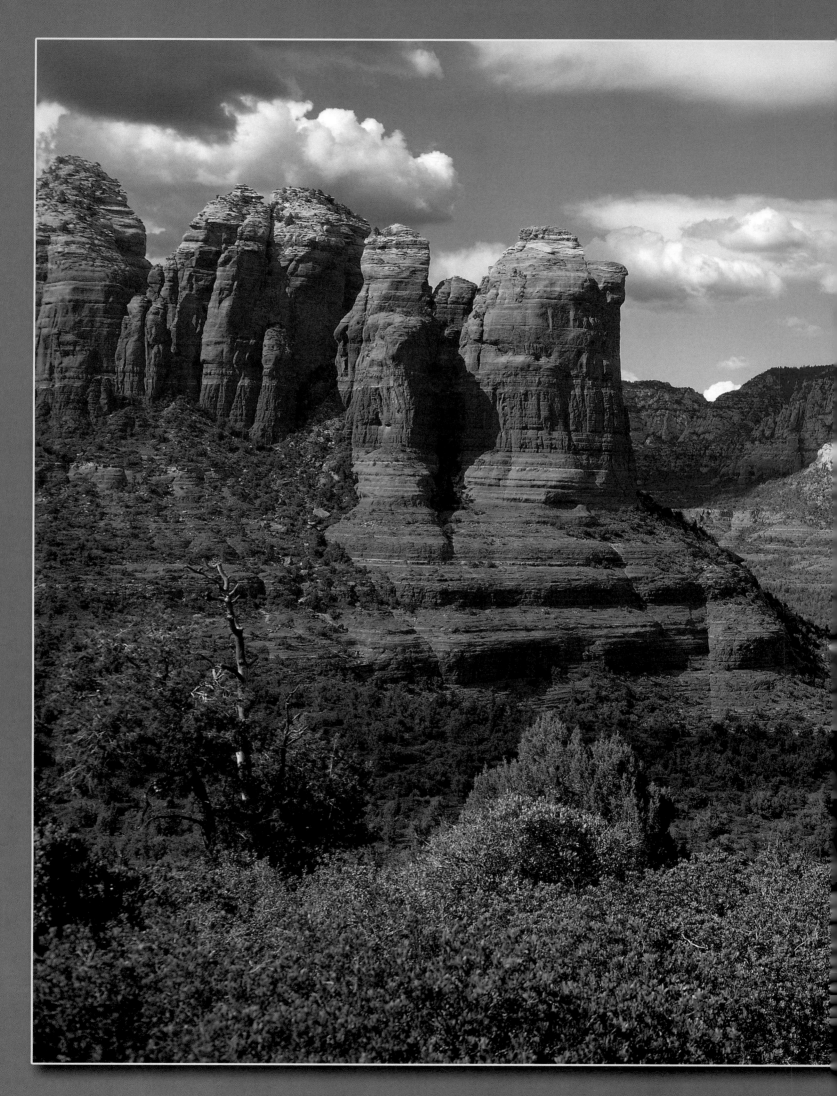

Coffee Pot Rock
in its splendor.

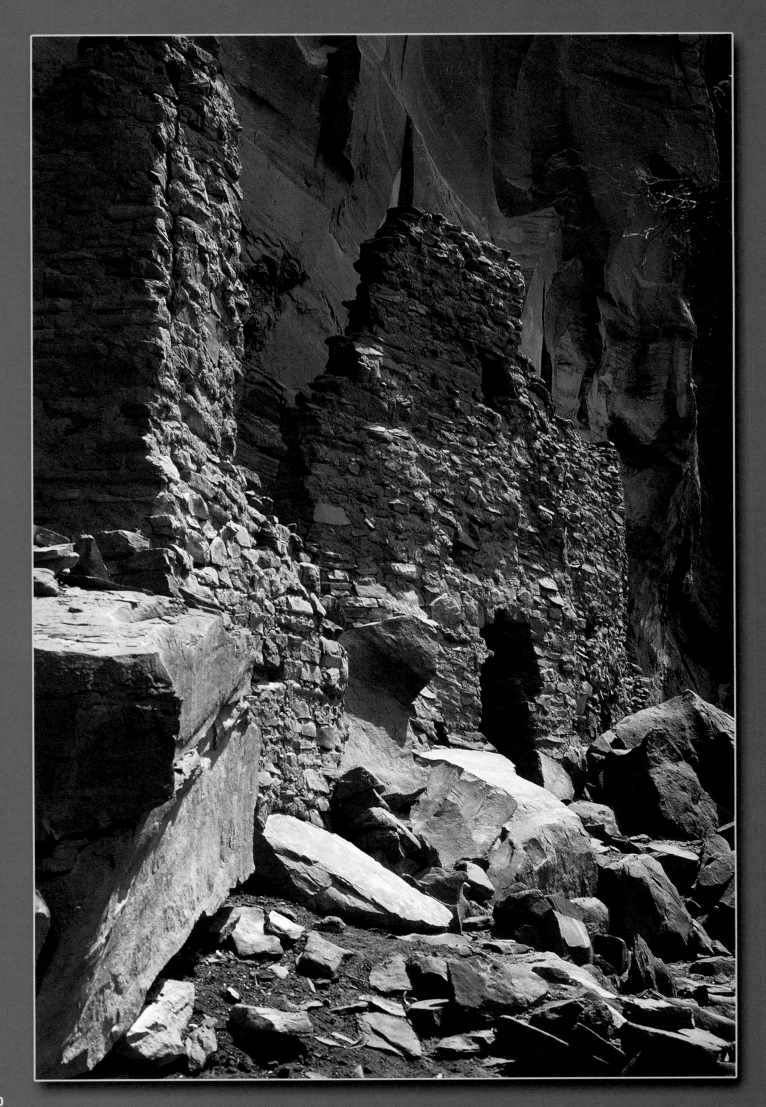

Left and above: Palatki Ruins

Hunanki Ruins

Pictographs and Indian ruins are in many of the canyons near Sedona.
In Boynton Canyon alone, there are over 50 ancient ruins – more than any other canyon.

The Chapel of the Holy Cross framed by the springtime bloom of narrow leaf yuccas.

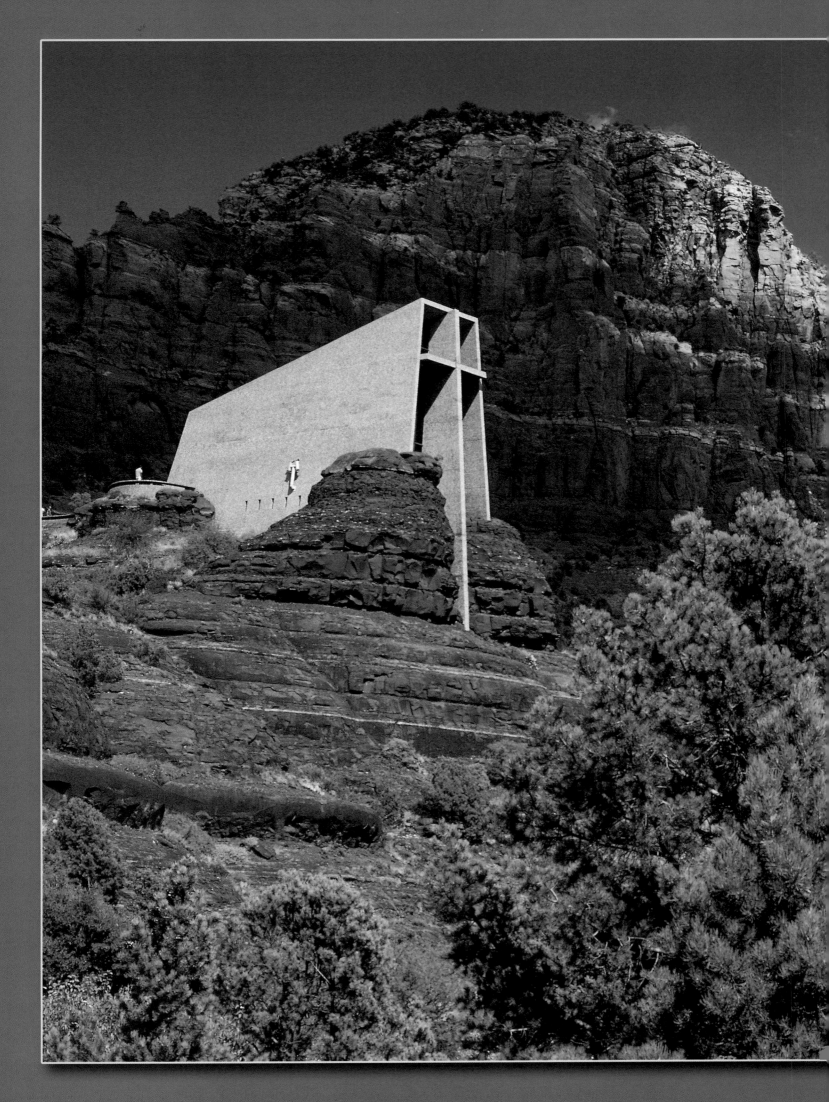

The Chapel of the Holy Cross attracts thousands of visitors to this part of red rock country.

Fay Canyon's
north end
presents views
of ponderosa pines
and red rock spires.

Schnebly Canyon displays its towering red rock walls.
Many of the red rocks in Sedona resemble wildlife.
This wall looks like a majestic eagle in flight.

Sedona red rocks
decorated by
drifting clouds
and fresh snowfall.

Oak Creek reflects
a winter scene of
Red Rock Crossing.

Boynton Canyon, west of Sedona, just after a January snowfall.